COURAGE

12 Best Practices to Advance Your Career

AMERICA BÁEZ CEDILLO

COURAGE
12 Best Practices to Advance Your Career

©Copyright 2023, America Báez Cedillo
All rights reserved.

No portion of this book may be reproduced by mechanical, photographic or electronic process, nor may it be stored in a retrieval system, transmitted in any form or otherwise be copied for public use or private use without written permission of the copyright owner.

It is sold with the understanding that the publisher and the individual author are not engaged in the rendering of psychological, legal, accounting or other professional advice. The content and views in each chapter are the sole expression and opinion of the author and not necessarily the views of Fig Factor Media, LLC.

Cover Design by Marco Alvarez
Layout by LDG Juan Manuel Serna Rosales

Printed in the United States of America

ISBN: 978-1-959989-50-9

To my parents, siblings, nieces and nephews. May my nieces and nephews find inspiration from this and chart their own paths. The sky used to be the limit, but not anymore. You can do anything you want if you set your mind to it. **You are loved and I believe in you!**

Table of Contents

Acknowledgments 5

Introduction 6

      Having Courage 8

      Having Faith 10

      It's All About Grit 12

      Personal Risks 14

      Professional Risks 16

      Learning to Adapt No Matter the Situation 18

      Set Your Intentions and Be Open-Minded 20

      How to Set Your Own Intentions 22

      Networking 24

      Tips for Successful Networking 26

      Your Journey to Having Courage 28

      Conclusion 30

About the Author 32

Acknowledgments

To my family, for always inspiring and motivating me to follow my dreams. Specifically, to my mom and dad, for your boundless energy, creativity, and passion in giving back to the community which helped guide me and encouraged me to be bold, creative, and ambitious toward my goals.

To my friends and colleagues who inspired and motivated me over the years. I could not have done this without their encouragement and support. They saw the limitless potential in me and pushed me to step out of my comfort zone.

I am grateful for having the opportunity to live the life I have, for being able to do what I am passionate about, and the chance to follow in my father's footsteps of becoming an author.

Introduction

Courage can be interpreted in many different ways. Having courage doesn't necessarily mean only speaking your mind, but also taking risks that are out of your comfort zone that can lead you to have better opportunities than before. It's about challenging yourself to take action and moving in the right direction instead of waiting for opportunities to come to you. This book will offer readers the chance to think about the concept of having courage in their personal and professional environments and how it can positively and negatively affect the outcome of their lives.

However, courage doesn't stand alone. Factors like having faith, grit, and the ability to adapt to new and uncomfortable situations are needed to fully comprehend the significance of courage. Furthermore, pursuing what you are passionate about is going to make all the difference and it's going to make life and work a fulfilling journey. By understanding the concepts within this book and applying them to your personal and professional lives, you will become more aware and will be more likely to succeed no matter where you are.

So, as you read through this book and learn to identify what it takes to have courage, and how it has impacted my life, I invite you to think about how you would apply it to your own situations. How can you use this book to achieve success?

COURAGE

COURAGE

Having Courage

To have courage is to make certain decisions without knowing the outcome. Many individuals believe that having the courage to confront obstacles will automatically end on a positive note, but in reality, that is not always true.

For instance, when a whistleblower has to make a decision to report an ethics violation at work, it could be terrifying for them to do so. They need to think about why they feel compelled to report this situation, and what their values are that make them think about doing this. Who is involved; how is this going to affect the company and their work; who is going to be impacted by this? What happens if this person doesn't report this situation? What are the consequences? Can this person live with this decision? Is this going to impact their work in the future?

These are the kinds of scenarios that we must prepare ourselves for when trying to muster up the courage to do something. It could be from doing simple things to making life-changing decisions, we must think of the consequences of not doing this and if we are comfortable with that, then it's okay. If not, we have to make a courageous decision and move forward.

COURAGE

Having Faith

HAVING FAITH

Having faith is another concept involved in mustering up the courage and taking risks is having faith. It's having a deep belief that things are going to work out. Whether you are a religious person or not, having faith pushes us forward believing that trusting this situation or decision will work out. Having faith gives us a strong foundation and belief that we can move forward with that idea or project and that things are going to have a positive outcome.

Whether we think of it or not, we exercise faith when making decisions, especially when encountering uncertain situations. It becomes more important when we intentionally incorporate it into our lives. We can influence the outcome of things with a positive attitude.

How can you intentionally start having faith in your life? Practice having faith when you are in any situation and would like a positive outcome. This will automatically make you feel better and it will help you deal with the outcome in a positive way.

Take time to reflect on this and think about a situation when you had faith even without you realizing it.

What was it and what did you learn from it?

Start envisioning a positive outcome every time by having faith and it will become part of your life.

COURAGE

It's All About Grit

We constantly face personal or professional challenges and we need to have grit to deal with them. We need to have the ability and strength of character to face setbacks in life. Not everything goes smoothly at work and we need to have grit to deal with disappointments and not let ourselves get demotivated. Instead, I count my blessings and I remind myself about things that I am grateful for and that helps me get through the disappointment.

In situations where the outcome is not what I wanted, I have learned to think that it's the universe redirecting me to better situations in life or career. For instance, I think of the challenging times when I was fighting my brain tumor and I instantly feel grateful for being alive and for getting another opportunity to try again. People notice this trait of yours when you have grit and you may gain more respect in their eyes.

Take time to reflect on this and think about a situation where you were disappointed. What was it and how did you overcome the disappointment? When faced with challenges, practice gratefulness and it will help you deal with them.

COURAGE

Personal Risks

PERSONAL RISKS

We get to a point in life that is all about taking risks. Every situation offers risks and rewards, and it is up to us to challenge the status quo and go for it.

I was planning on moving to the US to study English when I found out I had a brain tumor. Never in my life did I imagine I was going to have a brain tumor, especially in my mid-twenties. I was experiencing some symptoms and I went to see the doctor. After running a number of tests, I was diagnosed with a brain tumor. I remember the doctor telling me that I had a brain tumor and, depending on how it progressed, it could be very dangerous. I could lose my sight, I might not be able to have children, and, ultimately, I could die.

It was the scariest time of my life. I was totally shocked. I didn't know how dangerous this could be or where it was going to lead me. I had to take time to reflect on my situation and I decided to face it full-on and not let it stop me from following my dreams, as hard as that might be.

That is when I had to tell my parents that I was moving to the US (I had not told them up until that point) and that I had just been diagnosed with a brain tumor. The news was such a big blow to my parents, especially the latter one, of course. They wanted to know everything about my diagnosis and what I was planning to do. I told my parents that after learning of the diagnosis and talking to the doctor about a treatment plan, I had decided to still move to the US to study and move forward with my plans to eventually get a Master's degree.

COURAGE

Professional Risks

When I decided to build my own consulting and coaching business and speaking engagements after so many years of working in the corporate sector. It was a professional risk.

I looked at the pros and cons. I had great experience working with large companies, I had a great network and I had credibility, so that helped me make the decision to go for it. Some of the cons were whether I had enough funds to launch this business? Did I have the right business model and resources to succeed? I decided that I could work with experts to create the right business model and position myself for success.

This is an endeavor that I am still working at as I continue to build my business while still being part of the corporate world. I took a calculated risk and I had faith that it was going to work out, and it did.

COURAGE

Learning to Adapt
No Matter the Situation

LEARNING TO ADAPT NO MATTER THE SITUATION

We all go through different situations in life from when we are kids to growing up and going to college to when we start working. Moving from one situation to the next, from one place to another, we have to adjust to new conditions. Whether it is at home with family, at school, or at the workplace, we face different situations and people. We have to adapt to the new environment, the new way of doing things, new work styles, etc.

Going through the COVID-19 pandemic taught us that change is constant and that we need to learn to deal with it. We should expect the unexpected and prepare for it. Learning to adapt is key. Having the ability to change ideas or behaviors to adapt and evolve is critical for anyone trying to grow personally and professionally.

This is especially important when trying to advance one's career.

COURAGE

How to Set Your Own Intentions

- Remind yourself about your life goals. Think of how setting your intentions can affect them.

- Become familiar with the flow and general feeling of the room (new job, new boss, or any situation).

- Be strategic in how you approach the situation.

- Prepare for different situations and when faced with an unexpected one, think before you act.

- Set your intentions (list the steps to accomplish your goal).

Take a sheet of paper and answer these questions:

- What is the situation and what is your goal?

- Who and what is involved?

- How can you influence the situation or person to get a positive outcome?

COURAGE

Set Your Intentions and
Be Open-minded

Keeping your mind open to unexpected opportunities and situations can greatly benefit you. It's nature's way of challenging you to not be afraid of the possibilities that are out there.

When moving to a new job for instance, it is best if we go with an open mind—curious, interested in learning, and willing to adapt to the new culture and work style. Sometimes, when it is a new job, a new position, or a new boss, there might be some resistance to change. Although understandable, this may not be ideal if we want to succeed. We need to think and set our intention. Why are we here? What do we want to get out of this job? We need to observe, learn, and adapt to move forward in this new environment and be able to succeed.

Oftentimes, the most challenging part is getting along with colleagues. We must remain open to new people and situations, and not close ourselves off. It is best if we try to understand other people's backgrounds and perspectives and understand where we they are coming from. We especially must consider the end result if we want to stay in that job and succeed. Always keep an eye on the prize and do not let preventable things get in the way of your success. You could reach out to colleagues, get to know them, and build a relationship that will benefit you in your job. Most importantly, be yourself.

COURAGE

Networking

NETWORKING

In this complex world where things are changing fast, we need to learn to connect with people in a meaningful way. Whether it is at school, work, in the community, or virtually, it is important that we learn to network so that we can establish connections with people that might serve as a referral, etc. Networking is a two-way street. It is important that we spend time listening and getting to know the people in person or virtually. We can offer our assistance so that it is not just us reaching out to them at the last minute when we need something.

Networking at work is vital because it is going to help you potentially get on a new project or a new position, or introduce you to other opportunities. When working in large organizations, it is especially critical that you establish those connections that might give you referrals, recommendations, mentoring, or other work opportunities in the future.

If people don't reach out to you, reach out to them instead. Set up a meeting to learn about the person and think about what you can offer them—how you can assist them and nurture your network.

If you are looking for a new job, reach out to people in your network that might know someone working at the organization you are interested in. Once they make the introduction, you can ask them questions about the company, the culture, the job, and anything that might help you get your foot in the door.

Nowadays, networking applies to any situation. Remember, networking gets easier with practice.

COURAGE

Tips for Successful Networking

TIPS FOR SUCCESSFUL NETWORKING

As important as it is to know why networking is key, it's also important to know how to network. Connecting with others takes a strategy to match the energy of those you wish to connect with.

Follow these tips below to know how to successfully network:

- Identify organizations or people that will help you grow your network (i.e., professional associations, online networks, community organizations, schools, churches, etc.).

- Join the organizations and attend their events in person or virtually.

- Prepare your elevator speech (your name, title, what you do, and why you are attending the event in two minutes or less).

- Introduce yourself and reach out to people at an appropriate time to learn about them.

- Listen carefully and think about what you can offer that person.

- Establish a connection and start communicating with the person as appropriate (do not overdo it).

- Ask your friends or network for referrals or job leads in a respectful way.

- Nurture your network.

COURAGE

Your Journey to Having
Courage

It's important for you to identify your own journey to courage. Though the tips in this book will help you identify the different steps to having courage in your personal and professional life, it's up to you to make a change.

Answer these questions below:

- What is something that you would like to do and how can muster up the courage to do it?
- How is this going to benefit you?
- Do you have faith in this?

Then, take a sheet of paper and list the pros and cons of the situations where you are struggling to have courage in. Once done, analyze those with your answers to the questions above. What did you learn?

Conclusion

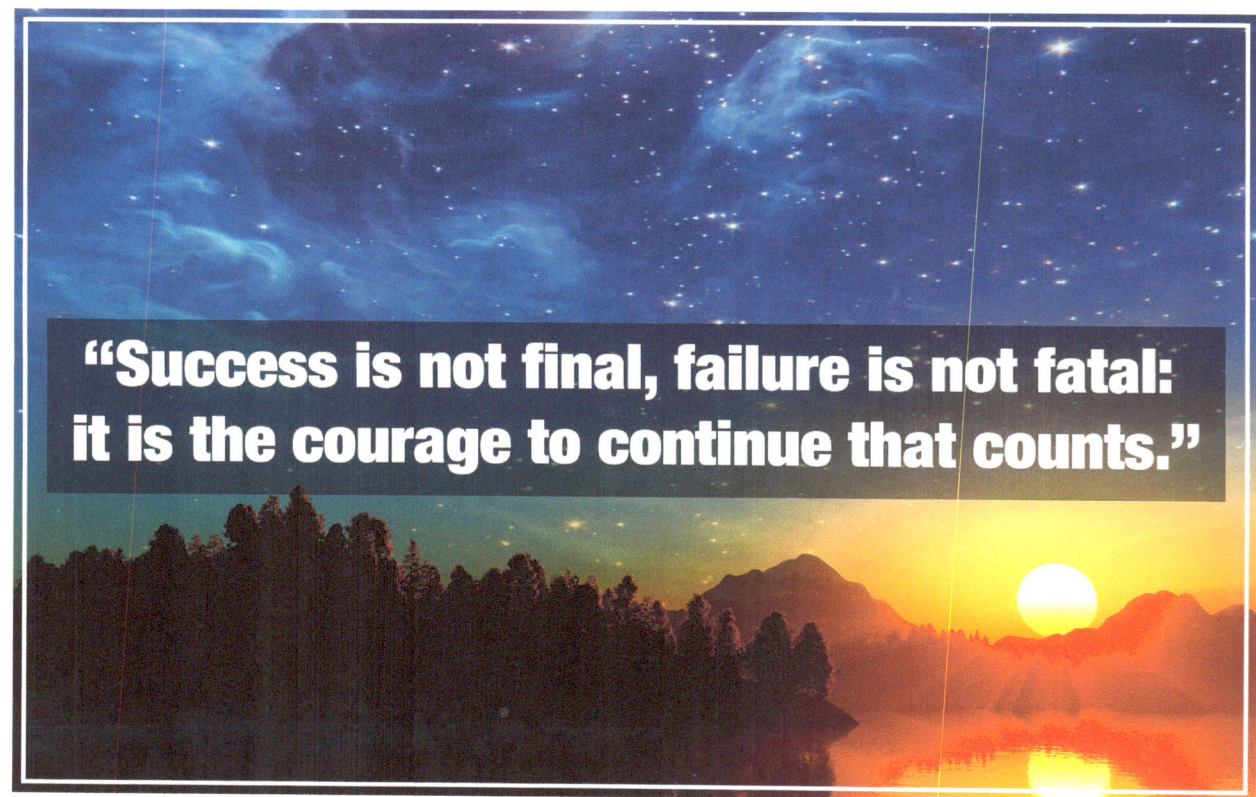

"Success is not final, failure is not fatal: it is the courage to continue that counts."

CONCLUSION

One of the most difficult parts of having the courage to do something is to know when you need to. As you face difficult situations that require you to have the courage to overcome them, remember that you are in control of the outcome. Take the lessons you have learned in this book and implement them into your own life and, most importantly, lead with courage and passion.

> *"If you have the courage to begin, you have the courage to succeed."*
>
> – HARRY HOOVER

CONCLUSION

About the Author

America Báez Cedillo has an extensive career as a global thought leader in talent acquisition and diversity, equity, and inclusion (DEI). She has implemented transformational global DEI talent solutions for Fortune 100 companies.

America Báez Cedillo is also a co-author of *Today's Inspired Leader Vol. 4*. Her chapter is titled: "Become the Leader You Are Meant to Be."

America grew up in Mexico in a family of teachers, politicians, artists, and poets who inspired her to follow her biggest dreams. She attended the Universidad Autónoma de Tamaulipas in Mexico and earned her MBA at Texas A&M International University. There she began a leadership journey that took her throughout corporate America while giving her a chance to uplift others, which is vital to her personally and professionally.

Connect with her via LinkedIn: America Baez

Visit her website: AmericaBaez.com

Printed in the USA
CPSIA information can be obtained
at www.ICGtesting.com
JSHW040733170923
48542JS00004B/8